YORKSHIRE 2001

Edited by

Heather Killingray

First published in Great Britain in 2001 by
POETRY NOW
Remus House,
Coltsfoot Drive,
Peterborough, PE2 9JX
Telephone (01733) 898101
Fax (01733) 313524

HB ISBN 0 75432 509 1
SB ISBN 0 75432 510 5

FOREWORD

Although we are a nation of poets we are accused of not reading poetry, or buying poetry books. After many years of listening to the incessant gripes of poetry publishers, I can only assume that the books they publish, in general, are books that most people do not want to read.

Poetry should not be obscure, introverted, and as cryptic as a crossword puzzle: it is the poet's duty to reach out and embrace the world.

The world owes the poet nothing and we should not be expected to dig and delve into a rambling discourse searching for some inner meaning.

The reason we write poetry (and almost all of us do) is because we want to communicate: an ideal; an idea; or a specific feeling.

Poetry is as essential in communication, as a letter; a radio; a telephone, and the main criterion for selecting the poems in this anthology is very simple: they communicate.

CONTENTS

THE POWER OF LOVE

She climbed mountains,
he climbed behind her,
she fought dragons,
he was her shield.

She was the rainmaker,
he was the spellbinder,
she was the moonlight,
he was the sunlight.

She was the clear waters,
he was the reflection in the stream,
she was the stepping stones,
he was the guiding light.

She was the child of the night,
he was the panther who stalked,
she was the eagle that flew,
he was the hunter that followed.

She was the jewel of the Nile,
he was the pilgrim who searched,
she was the sinner,
he was forgiveness.

She was his,
he was hers,
she would never regret,
he would never forget.

Rachel Henley (15)

LOVE IN PASSING

Our loved ones that have left this world,
are not so far away.
and though we grieve - we too believe
they're with us every day.

Our love must be our treasure,
and faith must be our guide.
And though we mourn - our hearts are drawn
forever, side by side.

Our comfort comes from loving,
from kindness and from prayer.
And though we weep - we'll always keep
the memories we still share.

Our love will be the Book of Life,
our thoughts and words the text.
And though we're weak - we still shall speak
in this world, and the next.

Our love then is the answer,
in every passing breath.
And though we cry - our love is why
In life, there is no death.

Rachel Mathers

OTHER SIDE

The other side is a place I've been,
It's a place I've been in my sleep,
In my sleep I drift away,
I drift away for another day,
For another day inside my head,
Inside my head where only I can tread,
Where only I can tread only I can see,
Only I can see deep within me,
Deep within me is a place I've been,
It's a place I've been where I've seen,
Where I've seen a million things,
A million things that are thoughts with wings,
Thoughts with wings that fly around,
Fly around without a sound,
Without a sound they explore my brain,
Explore my brain and bring joy or pain.

Graham Hyde

FOR SALE

For sale, two words so short, so sad,
No longer wanted, says the ad,
There is of course, a price to pay,
Call this number, without delay,
A bargain here, and no mistake,
To buy or sell, a profit to make,
A house, a car, a dream, a heart,
A vow that said, we'd never part,
Something happened along the way,
Whose fault was it, who can say?
It matters not, they are up for sale,
No one wants a sorry tale,
Only for gain, will they be sold,
The dream will die, and the heart grow cold,
There's more to this story, than meets the eye,
The house and the car, they do not cry,
But, maybe, just maybe, a new sale will be made
For the dream and the heart, hope must never fade,
The house and the car do not feel pain,
It's the dream and the heart that must live again.

Edna Hunt

SOULMATES

Health and happiness they all count
Towards the lifestyle that you want

So make sure you find the man
Who helps you become all you can

To help you grow and achieve your goals
A perfect match a meeting of souls

When you find him hang on tight
Never give him up without a fight

Show him love, don't be afraid and
Together your lives will be made.

M Temple

TO ERNIE WISE

Ernie Wise, you gave such
Delight to me, as a child,
When on your way to school,
You did the clog dance.
When you did pass the shops of three
Then on your hands you did walk with glee
All down the Grand View you did go
Right into the boys' school you did go.

Then to face your teachers you did go
Old Daddy Lodge you know
Or was it Freda Binks that you did see
Or Mrs Bennett to name but three
Mr Ingham was the headmaster you know,
You could tell such a tale of woe.

Mary Ackroyd

THE FIRE OF LOVE

Love is like a fire
A consuming burning desire
As it burns among the embers
The shame of it we remember.

Is it love that I feel?
Can it be real?
Or is it my imagination
And have I given it, creation?

It only takes a fool
To break love's golden rule
So if you know that love is wrong
Don't stay and get burnt, be strong.

What's not to be yours
You will never miss
So just keep clear
Of that cheating lover's kiss.

Don't be selfish
It could break your heart
For you and guilt
Will never, ever part.

Jean-Ruth

LUCY'S FRIEND

I've oft heard of Lucy Grey,
I know her storyline.
Orphaned at the age of three,
She was an only child.
Brought up by her aunt,
In a very old-fashioned way,
She never had any friends,
There was no one there to play.
When at last she started school,
At the tender age of five,
She found lessons so hard to learn,
Her plight no one could understand.
When children tried to befriend her,
She didn't know what to do.
She'd just sit there in the corner,
All alone and feeling blue.
At the end of the day her aunt would wait,
Standing there beside the gate
In a long black gown down to her toes,
No wonder the child was so confused.
One day her aunt was fully engaged,
Could no longer meet her there,
And standing at the gate instead,
Was a dog called Maisie May.
She accompanied her back home that night,
Became a familiar figure
Maisie May and Lucy Grey became inseparable,
And their way of life together was just incredible.
That day when her aunt passed away,
Maisie forever did with Lucy stay,
With such a loyal and faithful friend,
And this is where my story ends.

Joan Craven

THE MASKED GIRL

Soft toys and Barbie dolls,
The mask goes on . . .
Low-cut tops and lipstick.
'Ready or not, here I come -
Ring-a-ring o' roses . . .'
All fall down.

A wolf in sheep's clothing
Today invisibly integrated in
The City Centre.
The game continues.
'Eight, nine, ten!
Got ya!'
All fall down.

Esther Greenwood's fig tree
Suffocates the brain.
The ever-tightening grip . . .

Stop it!

All fall down.

Rebecca Culpan

CAPISTRANO . . . BAH 'T'AT!

Like the swallows me and Fred were heading for what the Yanks
call a little R&R
My tape to 'Teach yourself Italian' I'd played non-stop in the car!
Once there I'd eat real spaghetti and drink gallons of 'Vino Rosso'
Fred would demand meat and two veg, and tell Marco that his
Yorkshire puds were a bit flat and only 'so-so'!
I'd slap on suncreams and wear a posh sun hat. Fred would tie his
knotted hankie on his head ignoring the 'Panama' I'd bought
him and the sun's burning rays,
'I survived the sun in the Africa campaign, men were men
in those days!'
I'd dance the lambada with anyone willing and chat 'til the wee
small hours,
Fred now smothered in calamine lotion took lots of ice-cold showers,
saying he'd divorce me when we got home if I said once more
'Isn't it thrilling?'
I shopped 'til I dropped, he said I was reckless with my plastic,
'I'll not come abroad again,' he sighed, 'I'm past it.'
The days flew by, as I packed our bags to leave, I gave a sigh,
Fred was first on board that huge silver bird as it soared into the sky.
Back home now we sip a real cup of tea,
gazing contentedly at our Ilkley Moor,
Fred's right, well on this particular score,
'No place on earth to beat this' as he puffs away at his pipe
ignoring the dark skies threatening from a distance,
The big daft lummox with his head still red-raw, he thinks I don't
see him give a secret wince
'Best be heading home Lass,' as he points to the ominous
black clouds yonder!

I love these moors with their violence and beauty,
a place to come to regain my strength, as I quietly pack away
the picnic hamper I ponder,
Do the swallows long to see familiar sights when they return to foreign
shores? For if they do, then they're like me, for absence does make the
heart grow fonder.

J M Hefti-Whitney

TIME OCEAN

Time is a drop in the ocean my friend.
Those that you know will soon be gone.
It'll be hard to swim against the tides,
The sea will wash away your dream castles.

Time is a drop in the ocean, my friend
The words that you never said
will swim away,
Those that you never went to see,
will drown forever,
The ships on their return smashed
upon the rocks.

Time is a drop in the ocean my friend.
Cast your nets far and wide to catch the sea,
Sail to the coastlines of those that wait for you.
Ride the waves, catch what you can and
remember well,
Time is a drop in the ocean, my friend
Time is a drop in the ocean, my friend.

Roman Suchyj

THE PURPLE ROSE

'I don't like it,' the girl said
Aware she was naked
Under the white sheet her body spread,
It didn't feel soft like at home.
She felt fear but couldn't understand why?
It took my breath away
The reluctant tone of his voice
When the man pronounced me dead!
Gripped by a sudden spasm
Swimming a purple rigid sea.
Her body shook, then relaxed, so relaxed
Her heart beating ultramarine tranquillity.
Where am I going? She heard the voice
'Walk into the light!'
She could feel her legs again.
Naked she walks feeling the brightness
Engulfing body and mind
Warm and welcoming neon lightness.
A spore in the cosmic flow
Dragged against the pull of its tide
A cerulean shadow.
Pierced by a single memory seeping
Only once. Her mind absorbed,
She lay, dream sleeping.
At one with the universe and its God
Unaware of the cold steel
And freezing fog.

Mary Jane Evans

A WINTER'S DAY IN THE PENNINES

It was snowing
Soft flakes fell upon me
And our world was white,
The hills around us looked beautiful.
It was bitterly cold.
Not the cutting blast of the high ground
But the penetrating chill of valley and river,
The stunted trees grotesque
Branches heavy with snow
And devoid of foliage.
The sky hung like a pall
Over the bleak scene
And the snow got thicker.
The church clock struck three
Soon the day would meet the long night.
A little boy, face pressed to a cottage window
Smiled and waved, and to me the sun came out.

E M Pucknell

MY HOME TOWN
(Goole, East Yorkshire)

Green fields, by a muddy, lazy river flowing by,
Farms, cottages, a windmill's sails against the sky,
Man-made river to divert high tide's flow,
Wild fowl, fens and marshes, golden sunset glow.
A canal was dug to join towns, rivers and sea,
Houses were built, docks were made, a new town came to be.
Aire Street, North Street, Boothferry Road too,
Banks Hotel, North Eastern Railway, a town all new.
The docks expanded, the little town spread,
A railway network, many ships, busy times ahead.
A bustling little port, a market town, grew more and more,
Shops were opened, businesses too, new folk by the score.
It survived the wars, not unscathed, but still on the map,
The motorway arrived, with a new bridge, no looking back!
Yet suddenly it seems, our town has gone slowly down,
Shops and businesses closing, not so many jobs around.
We're being pedestrianised and I truly hope that
This will put our businesses firmly in the black,
For Goole is home to me, although I've lived away,
I've always returned to my little home and here I plan to stay.
I really hope that good times will return here again
For the decline of Sleepy Hollow causes me much pain.
I had such good times here when I was young,
We didn't need to go very far looking for fun.
Others may call it and try to pull it down
But to me it will always be my home town.

Christine Naylor

PAPERCHASE

I deem this game the Paperchase
A literary competition
Running through the alphabet
A phonetic expedition

A dyslexic person's nightmare
An author's life's desire
Where publishers have the final say
The editor playing umpire

Dialect, accent and grammar
Are obstacles to be overcome
The acne of the erudite world
An illiterate's mansion

For the poetic paperchase
Has no rules and regulations
You write how you write, and spell how you spell
Use any connotations

The world of words is a giant place
A place that holds no bounds
Where all words have a meaning
All proverbs, verbs and nouns.

Claire Piwowarski

AUTUMN

At the end of this autumn day,
I feel a great sense of peace.
As I peer through my small window,
I can almost smell the fragrant leaves covering my
pathway. Berries glow in the hedgerows, letting me know
of their presence, only to be admired.
These golden days, not to be missed, but to be savoured
throughout the winter months.
And next year at this time, long forgotten, the surprise of
it all, yes, they're here once more, the golden days.

Carole O'Neil

TO CHARLOTTE

Do the wild windswept moors
Call to you, in the darkest hours?
Do they send their friend the wind
To bring you back to them again?

A bleak landscape of grass and heather
Where you and your sisters, walked together
Dreaming of a life, you were never to know
Did you talk about the places, you would like to go?

Though in your grave you lie
You have not been forgotten with time
You still live on, in people's hearts
With admiration for your works.

Happiness, seemed to delude you, most of your life
Except for a few months, when you became a wife
But then my assumptions, are from what I have read
By people who wrote about you, when you were dead.

Oh, I know you loved the moors
The howling wind, held no fears
Was it a comfort to your ears
As you wiped away your tears?

Linda Tosney

SEASIDE DEBUT

Reminiscing with a smile my snaps,
my first ever visit to the seaside,
Bridlington in June.
Odours of fish swept by the breeze,
caress my nose to prove I am here.

Above the harbour hover seagulls,
in anticipation of scraps discarded
by thoughtless tourists,
Fish, cockles and mussels, are sold on
every street corner.

Trips upon the sea depart every hour,
should I partake?
No! I'd be seasick I'm sure.
Fishing boats laden with the day's catch
litter the quayside.

Peering down at the quayside's edge,
I fall in (typical!)
Striving ferociously to be salvaged
I beckon unto the ogling fishermen
laughing at their daily catastrophe.

Onto the quayside I embarrassingly arrive,
attired as heavy as lead.
Saturated, my twenty-pound hair-do
reduced to an image of Worzel Gummidge
as I squelch embarrassingly away.

Suddenly halted by my saviour
who places in my hand
a giant muscle shell,
to commemorate - apparently - christened,
my unsavoury seaside debut.

Steve Kettlewell

PHILOSOPHY

Don't just sit there, thinking, of the things you'd like to do,
Maybe when you have some time to spare, say, in a year or two.
For who knows what fate may have in store, if you'll be fit or no,
Dreams can only come true, if you do things now, and so
Enjoy what each day has to offer, take your chances whilst you may,
Yesterday has gone, tomorrow uncertain, you only have today!

Kathleen Adams

COMMITTED

Iron-bound yet slack of jaw,
a shell that breathes still,
body gone and mind no more
upright through sheer will.
Roped together and armour-plated,
smashed yet held and true,
pride entangled with hope belated
all that tethers you.
Knock it down and be no longer
rise and take a fall,
know it now and be the stronger
no one can win them all.
Tearing limbs of proven mettle
or breaking vows of stone,
will make no odds as all things settle
and find us all alone.
However tied to those unwilling,
beyond the chains and fetters,
lies the truth that is in truth killing,
freedom beckons if only we'd let us.

M J Morris

SNAILS

They marched in silence through the night
A hidden army in pale moonlight,
Their sticky batons stretched and waved,
Their carriage shells smoothed and swayed.
Slowly they scaled paver and brick,
One foot infantry secret and slick.
Tiny curls on caps were scattered,
Trails of silver on patio spattered.
A watchful hedgehog winked an eye
And crunched its jaws as they passed by.
Fifty or more there must have been
On dewy grass, on lawn, on green,
Towards the house like a magnet drawn
Pushing and pushing the calling dawn.
Mysterious army the sun has shone . . .
How did you know . . .?
Where have you gone . . .?

Christine Williams

WARNING GIRLS, ON THE SEVENTH DAY GOD INVENTED FOOTBALL

Beware, that special breed of man.
The avid Sunday football fan
Whose idea of fun is to follow West Ham
Best say goodbye now, whilst you can.

For once you lose your heart to him
You'll lose your Sundays for your sin
Football's a game that's always *in*
Best learn to lace the flask with gin.

Each weekend is the same routine
Up at eight, where're you've been
The night before, you watch *The Team!*
Support them 'till they reign supreme.

Life is planned around training nights
Nothing stops those football tykes
The game is all, you have no rights
You thought support, referred to tights!

Grasp quickly girls the football term,
Offside, man-on, push up - you'll learn!
He takes a knock, that makes you squirm
A cosy fire is what you yearn.

What friendly lads make up the team
A win! Their crimson faces beam
Contentment, true we are the cream!
It really wasn't just a dream.

We've won *The Cup* - sweet victory!
It's hugs all round and shouts of glee!
Lady Luck at last has come to tea
You're hooked - you should have heeded me!

Sharon Stead

WHO'S OLD?

In my mind I am not old
I have colour in my hair.
My skin is smooth and wrinkle free
for I haven't got a care.

The mirror tells the truth though,
the years have not been kind.
The silver strands and creases,
a face that's worn and lined.

Still my memory is quite good,
I can remember long ago.
Places I have been to
and names that I still know.

But I don't always know what day it is,
they seem to run together.
And things they seem to move themselves
I'm getting to the end of my tether.

I try and see others points of view
although I don't agree.
I'm sure that society's getting worse,
it can't just be me!

They say that wisdom comes with age
I'm sure that can't be true
That would mean I'm getting old.
Do I look old to you?

Sharon Tyler

IN FLANDERS FIELD

Asleep they lie they cannot feel
The kiss of the sun to warm and heal
Their manhood lost in a foreign land
No one to keep the warrior band
But poppies red adorn the grave
Of the deathless ones
The sons of the brave
Those that we have loved and lost
At what dreadful cost
Still linger in our hearts today
They are never far away
No, we shall not forget
We shall remember them

Olive Winkworth Ullah

TO RETIRE

To retire in military terms
Is to retreat from enemy arms
But many a battle has been won
By a retreat that was just a *come on.*
Now I have retired
But not in a military sense.
I'm over the age of sixty-five years
On a pension of eighty pounds and a few pence.
My battle now is against ill health
Boredom and lack of wealth.
In the face of these foes
To fall back is not on
To the death the fight goes
Till the battle is won.
My life I've enjoyed these many years
Despite times of fear and shedding of tears.
I owe so much to so many
Debts I can never repay
I shan't die rich in money
But a millionaire in a way.

J H Ainsworth

THE LOST BONUS

Tom arrived late on Monday morn
With stooping shoulders and face forlorn
Said Tom 'I've had an awful fright
Attacked by dog which tried to bite.'
A big black dog in search of meat
Grabbed hold of trousers in the street,
Tom took to his heels and flew
Closely followed by the grew
When Tom stopped running, to his dismay
He found he'd finished down Elder Way
Cried Tom 'I'm in an awful fix!'
The reason - he'd not clocked on for six!

C W Edwards

HAPPY BIRTHDAY TO THE IMMORTAL ONE

Does it matter that death becomes him,
Worn lightly, if worn at all,
Could we ever pin its rosettes upon him
When his presence was a mirage to us all.

And now a mirage of respectability
Atop a world of unremitting grey
Of polluted hopes and tight little dreams,
And pitch dark nights that muffle screams.

This is why those who remember
How the Carnival died in the dust,
In that arena of exquisitely planned cabaret,
Know that this is only the dawning
Of what may always be a happy/sad day.

We may think when he becomes visible,
At the twilight of his *distinguished* life,
Time may cheat us of our ceremony,
As death steals him from our embrace;

But does it matter how death becomes him
As long as the carnival of doubt begins,
As he sits himself, in a darkened room
And an unfamiliar night draws in.

So whilst his thoughts may never match ours,
And his confinement is in a comfort of which we'd never dream,
As long as this carnival of doubt prevails
May we finally say a karmic *Amen?*

J A Clark

OUR LIFE'S MEMORIES

We sat under this apple tree when I
got down on one knee
and asked you to marry me.

Oh it was woe as you announced
we were wed
as you rested your weary head into bed

Our lifestyle has been a bit of a muddle
a lot of trouble to say the double
But it beats being a tearaway Jack
as I pile everything into this sack.

Kids - we have had them and more by the score
As you toured about on a faraway shore
are you sure it was love or a dream from afar
or notes that sounded from an old glass jar
that said it wasn't for me.

But every footstep and every echo
in the darkness of night
lets me hold on tight until the morning light
As delightful shadows dance on the windowpane.

But it's not love and we're not insane
As our love is moving once more
It's such a bore that life cannot
be here from eternity.

A Renyard

RUDSTON

When arms grew weak
Rome kept her power by other means.
By Saints.
A bloody, eastern rebirth cult
Came in like laurels, rabbits, plumbing . . .

Beside Rudston Church a stone stands proud
Heaviest granite lifted high in weightless form
Angle-edged perfection, dove-tailing earth to sky
Dead-eye central to the mound
The dale, the earth, the great beyond

It is said a turncoat pagan priest
Coifi, not a Michael or a George,
Speared the old religion dead
Circled the magic hill three times
Before he lanced his own god's statue down.

Now, on first foundations
A Norman tower squats.
Did clever Coifi lance with a smile?
While the stone is intrinsic, full of guile
The church is off-set, forever misaligned.

Peter Ardern

TO EVERYONE WHO HAS LOST SOMEONE

We all know it's heartbreaking to lose someone,
Whether it is an animal or a part of your human family
But what we all must understand is that they now thrive in Heaven,
And are looking down on all of us, smiling happily.
I know you think it's just a cliché and has all been said before,
But it's wrong to recall their drastic ending as death closed life's doors.
Instead, imagine a whispering waterfall that swept peacefully through
their eyes,
A sweet lullaby that hushed them to sleep and melted the pain of
death's cold ice.
It's good to grieve, so let out all of your tears,
Remember them for the wonderful life they led
Even if it's one of your worst fears . . .
To hear the news that they are dead.
I know it's hard, so hard to stop crying,
I know you feel hopeless, as if you'll never get through
I understand you so want to join them by dying,
But believe me, when this happens, everyone feels the same too.
Talk to them through your prayers every night,
Show them your feelings, tell them you miss them
For now they are bathed in a heavenly light,
And one day, on some shore, you'll meet again.
But until then, you have all of your life to live,
You have love to receive and kindness to give
But never forget that special member of your family,
For they'll never forget you . . .
Smiling down from Heaven happily.

Natalie Dybisz (14)

FRIENDSHIP

F   riends are indispensable
R   egard them with loyalty and affection
I   dentifying a friend is when you can call up at 2am
E   ven if a friend is powerless, it's enough to know they exist
N   ever take them for granted
D   o we deserve such friends!
S   haring both our joys and sorrows
H   aving a friendship like this means the world to me
I   feel privileged to have the comfort of friendship
P   erhaps I'm one of those lucky ones.

Donna Crocker

MIST

Coming from nowhere, mist drifts with the breeze.
Mist is damp, it's deadly and feels wet on your skin.
Bringing cold to your bones, starts your breathing to wheeze.
You will know it's within, as you start to sneeze.
Pain starts in your head and your eyes become dim.
Coming from nowhere mist drifts with the breeze
Dripping with wet as you begin to freeze.
Your skin becomes pale like that of white satin.
Bringing cold to your bones, causing your breathing to wheeze.
The wandering mist, wet and dripping from trees.
Staying with you, although it is unwell you are getting.
Coming from nowhere, mist drifts with the breeze.
Bringing aches and pains and nothing to please.
Starting to regret that mist that was wetting.
Bringing cold to your bones, worsening your breathing to wheeze.
From the illness you feel, starts a desire for release.
A short time passes and you are deceased.
Coming from nowhere, mist drifts with the breeze.
Bringing cold to your bones, mist caused your breath to wheeze.

Harry Eastwood

I Am What I Am
'I Am Me'

I am unique
I am what I am
I am 'John Gaze'
Nothing more, nothing less
I was born to be me.

I am no-one else's creation
No-one else's puppet
No-one else's slave

My smell, my touch, my needs, my wants
my goals, my dreams they are all parcelled up in me

The salty tears, the sadness, the years in the wilderness where I was
continually drunk with pain, *not earned* but inherited, guilt upon my
shoulders from clumsy souls
who bore me no good.

The role, the part I played for years (the script all too garbled for me)
a mantle of perfection, I could not play anymore.
I let roll off my shoulders.

I cannot play 'Jesus Christ' anymore, nothing more, nothing less.
I'm too human for that. I want to be me - no more roles to play.
I just long for one person to fit this physique. Just one person, just me.

I am unique
I am what I am
I am 'John Gaze'
Nothing more, nothing less
I was born to be me.

John Gaze

JOURNEY

Step into the night we'll find the light together if we try.
Look to the sail to catch the breeze to guide us to the Milky Way.
Search for the stars on the way, we'll always be a million miles away
But together in a special way,
And when we arrive we'll have just begun.
Now we must come together as one.

Andrew Welburn

A TERRIER'S LESSON
(Aromatherapy)

Fragrance fills the airways
and adheres to all around.
Angus loves the mornings
and the fresh smells on the ground.
He leads his little protégé
through the early morning dew
And from the misty, purple peaks,
they stand and marvel at the view.

For this is the land of Angus
with its heather and its pines,
These are the streams, the very lifeblood,
of those 'special' Highland wines.
The smell of fresh-cut Scottish peat
does oft-times assail the air,
Angus feels his hot blood rush
as once more his nostrils flare.

He scents a stag and off he bounds
to chase the Monarch of the Glen,
Ailsa, his wee protégé, hesitates
but soon is off again.
Leaping, striding, bounding,
side by side they run,
Who'd have thought a lesson in aromatherapy
would turn out to be so much fun?

Loyd Burt

STOP AND SAY HELLO

No pity, don't patronise, just say hello
To the figure you see in the chair.
Slumped to one side, head falling low
Appearing to be in despair.

This was once a vibrant being
Enjoying life and living.
Parties, holidays, sunshine and skiing
Career building, unforgiving.

Never a thought about next year
Of what may await in life.
Never a risk as no sense of fear,
Living on the edge of a knife.

Spring and summer had run their length.
Some friends didn't make the grade
Which reminded of mortality's strength
Too late, destiny was made.

Years slid past, time moved on,
Then days struggled in dawning.
Once bright eyes became dulled in the sun,
This became the season of mourning.

Now I watch those in this place
Whose charge is my well-being.
Everything's done at too fast a pace,
They're looking but they're not seeing.

Don't dismiss me, my life's been full
Of memories both high and low
Don't condemn me to days that are dull,
Spare time, stop and say hello.

Franklin H Smith

WHEN WILL THIS HAPPEN?

As I wander down the village street under a cloudless sky
I gaze at the garden all so neat and see the cars go by
I think of how it used to be when we first arrived
Of all the peace and quiet that has not survived
I see vandalised benches and open trenches
And new road being made
And more and more plans for houses being laid
It used to be two villages, Brough and Elloughton
But now it's got so large it seems like only one
The roads that used to be so quiet, tranquil, comatose
But now we've got estates no one even knows
And another one is on the way the problem's going to be
I wonder will we see the day when we can't find a tree
Accept by walking out into the hills and dales
That's if they survive the purchases and sales
Of the human urge for profit and oft wanting more
Then these two villages will be a town of that I'm sure.

Ray Blythe

FORGET-ME-NOTS

Once we were flesh, blood, muscle and bone
Now we're just names on a list carved in stone
Once we touched, heard, spoke and were seen
Now we're just the dust of what might have been.

Once we lived, breathed, had thoughts in our head
Now we're just symbols of a flower blood-red
Once we left loved ones broken-hearted,
                    from their lives we had departed.
Now they too have long since gone
In strangers' memories we must live on.

Once we died so you could be free
Faced the gunfire, felt the shots
Now we must remain in your memory
For we are the forget-me-nots.

Paul Windley

Oh To Find Beauty In A Garden Of Thorns

From behind the bushel of the thorny rose, came the light of true
friendship - the sword of hope,
She walked as an angel through the mists of time strong and clear,
She looked at me deeply and we introduced ourselves again
For far away in the dawn of an age, we met once before and
then over again.

The thorns they did rip me and tear at my face
But the fire burned bright and guided my way
The strength from her smile, the pull from way down
The eyes so familiar, the soul I once knew well
The tug of minds together, powers combined, consciences unified.

I lay at your feet my lady of fire, though I fight to reach your heart
The tower through the thorn walls and the dragon's flame
The highest of the windows the most treacherous the path
Till I find the question asked and the immediate answer

For blood may well tie us and spells cast us tight
The magic is in endurance and the beat of our hearts
We Witches of Endor, we two of bright power,
Together we are indestructible, 'gainst whomever we fight
My witch lady friend, my lady of the night
I give you my hand.

Emma Bannister

ANTHEM - PEARL WEDDING - 2ND AUGUST '99

Do you remember when we were giants
with shoulders that held up the sky,
the world at our feet for the taking
if we only wanted to try.

Now I'm sitting and enjoying a pint
with some old and very dear friends
and I'm seeing things a little differently
from much nearer life's other end.

I never climbed any mountains
there'll not be a book of my life
just a humdrum existence
two children, a mortgage, a wife.

But you were always beside me
as I floundered along through life's race
always there to support me
as I slipped ever nearer last place.

There've been many times full of laughter
and not a few times I nearly cried
and I know to the world I'm a failure
but you know how hard I tried;

And I still remember when we were giants,
when we knew we could have it all,
before life and reality intruded
dashing some hopes to the wall.

T Ireland

AEROBICS CLASS

Grapevine
Bottle of wine
Two scoops
Ice cream
Bicep curls
Viennese whirls
Heel toe
Chocolate gateau
Swivel your hips
Plate o' chips
Spotty dog
Hot dog
Easy step
French baguette
In twos
Plenty of booze
Four more
Just pour
Last eight
Empty the plate
Heel digs
Syrup o' figs

Christine Gillet

E TENEBRIS LUX (OUT OF DARKNESS, LIGHT)

What of the valley now the mines have gone?
What of the people who have to carry on?
Gone are the head stocks, the chimneys and the tips
Gone are the railroads, the wagons and the skips.

Deep underground, the silent caverns stand
But though the rocks by man's determined hand
Highways and byways down which the coal was brought
Destined for furnace, for homestead and port.

Down in the darkness, there is no day or night
Never again the smallest spark of light
Never more a footfall, or a spoken word
Where once was noise and bustle, there's nothing to be heard.

Left as an underworld, that none shall see again
Sealed like a tomb, forever to remain
A subject of legend and failing memory
Part of our folklore to be, eventually.

What of men who laboured in the mine?
As they grow old their stories will decline
Tales of disasters of strikes and honest toil
Now all replaced by natural gas and oil.

Janet Cavill

PRIORITIES

I do not need money, power and glory
To make me feel happy and alive
I do not need to drink alcohol to give me confidence
Just the love of my wife and two kids

My hands do not tremble for the need of a cig
And I certainly do not need drugs to give me a kick
I do not need a mansion to live in
Just the love of my wife and two kids

I do not need two cars to go to work in
Just one will do for me
I do not need spin doctors telling me what to do
I have my wife and we will do what we want to do

So all in all I thank our God
My wife and children too
For filling my life with love and loyalty
Making me happy and content too.

Hetty Foster

KINGSTON-UPON-HULL

Welcome to the city of crowns
A place of heritage and high renown
Feel the strength in this sprawling town
Made even stronger by the walls taken down

We hope you like your stay
And want to come back soon
If you wish to bring a friend you may
We will try to find you rooms

Behold this fair place
Ancient city of the King
Please accept our warm embrace
As your time with us begins

May your visit to our city
Be made worth your while
By warm, friendly faces
And real Yorkshire smiles.

C J Collins-Reed

TOO MANY DAFFODILS

'Enough of daffodils!' she said,
Complaining to the local press
After the winter cold and drear
With bitter cold and dismal wet.
And even now the rain persists
Though springtime's long
Officially here.

Through the damp mists triumphantly,
Emerge, defiant, jocund heads
Of countless yellow daffodils
By ancient walls, in gardens,
Under trees.
A reminder of the hidden sun,
Of quickening life, renewal, hope
In York's fair city.

So anyone who cannot see
These signs in every proud array,
This wealth of gold, this treasure trove,
Must be deserving of our pity.

Can there ever really be
Too many daffodils?

Jacqueline Abendstern

Zoos

You go to the zoo if you have children to take,
Mostly take a picnic and some cake,
A lot like the performing seals,
You can often see them having their meals.

Lions and tigers are kept in a cage,
Wouldn't like to see them in a rage.
Children can have elephant rides,
While the zebra has stripes down its sides.

The different bears can give you a fright,
While wallabies romping is a grand sight.
Monkeys do have really funny ways,
While children drive parents in a daze.

Pamela J Earl

OBSESSION

The yellow orchid of your dreams.
Shadows that frighten at dawn,
Its strange electric glow
Of soft pink clouds.
Chase away the doldrums
With my humdrum beat,
Whispers cold greetings
To the lovesick heart,
Take advantage of the lovelorn.
And yellow blossoms
Into white lilies fade, sweet nectar
Tormented by their tricky poison.
A cock crowed to end the day
The second trumpet blast, from Revelation
Speaks. But saxophones and drums
Are what lulls me to sleep.
Its purple calyx, its black stamens
Caress my cheek.
I wash my hair
With emptiness; and shower in despair
With worn soap its cracked essence
Of fading memories, refreshes.
Music is my love - feed me
Play on; dreaming hi-fi dreams.
Touch me, touch my soul,
Touch me deep
Its sweet rhythms
Soothe the brain; stimulate sleep.
A scented minim on your pillow
An octave from your
Rocking glass mirror.

A double cleft in your heart
Its melody never dies
Beating in your breast
Of rainbow-flowered skies.
Beats forever autumn
Comes again in the morning
Its sweet music's gentle refrain.

Mary-Jane Evans

UNTITLED

'Ever dance with the Devil by the pale moonlight?'
Said one clown to another in the dead of night.
These clowns were sworn enemies by nature and name
The good guy, the bad guy, both twisted the same.
Pure good, pure evil, the most dangerous mixture
The rabbi, the gangster, the jailer, the trickster.
One reeking havoc through the city
With his noxious cash and foul ditty
The other had to clean up all he'd done
Staring down the barrel of his gun
Not once but twice in his lifetime
Had he committed such a crime
The first one was so long ago
When the blood was red against the snow
The eyes were cold, the clenched fist gloved
One pull of the trigger, he lost all he loved.
Never would he forget the face
Never would he give up the chase
When he saw the face once more
Down below on the factory floor
He dipped it in a vat of pain
Never would it be the same again
No riddle me this or riddle me thats
No deadly umbrellas or bowler hats
Revenge. It's the one unspoken word
That does not pass by the pair unheard.

Above the sleeping city, the two meet alone
One will fly high, the other sink like stone.
On tarnished rooftops drawn together
To end this lifelong feud forever.

Joanne Starkie

STROKE VICTIM

A tempest had burst one day
without any early warning,
its thunderclap wreaking
destruction that couldn't be healed,
a wasteland without any hope -
the certainty death would be better.

Any attempt to lengthen life
was vain and the best course to take
looked plain. Let him slip away
in comfort, see to his bodily cares,
turn him once every two hours,
bathing him in bed, give him paracetamol.

His meagre nutrition was liquid
through a needle stuck into his skin.
His head was supported by pillows,
the hospital linen was crisp.
As the ward went about its routine
his bed was concealed by a curtain.

Shut like a shroud the curtain
hid the dying man from sight.
The doctor watched over his charge.
The spectacle too ghastly and sad
to be glimpsed by other patients -
his face a paper mask, the spirit almost gone.

The nursing staff always stayed calm -
fulfilled what was needed with skill,
their telephone manner kept cool.
A whole week passed, but he lived,
his family visited, grieved,
fought one against the other - then he died.

Peter Cardwell

HOPE OUT OF DESPAIR

(For Askern)

My grandson's shrieks echo in the silence,
Bouncing off loose corrugated metal.
'High in the sky,' he shouts excitedly.
'Look out, Nanna, we'll soon be going down!'
I pretend it's a rollercoaster, whilst
Stepping precariously over the cracks.

I explain, beneath The Plant Bridge men worked,
Converting coal to coalite from The Pit.
No men now, just alien landscape.
A slight smell of sulphur pervades the air.
Gone are the wagons, once bearing products
Of our men's toil and sweat, their jobs lost.

Graffiti-painted bricks on the slopes' walls,
Dodging a pool of water when it rains,
My grandson and I make a game of it.
Down Chapel Hill we enter 'The Dark Wood'.
Entwining branches form a canopy,
Captivating wildest imaginings.

Shops boarded up, struggling, many for sale,
With shutters to keep out vandalism
They promise us parks, more houses - for whom?
Who would want to build or settle here now?
'What is behind the high wall?' he asks me.
'I don't know,' never wondered or enquired.

Yet he does, which enlivens, stirs my heart.
He has no memories of what I knew,
He does not grieve for what was and is gone.
Our grandchildren will build, and start anew,
Their children will find fulfilment once more:
My hope rekindled, something to strive for.

Janet Hewitt

THE CLOCK

I sat in the chair
By the clock on the wall
That ticks away hours
And stops not at all.

As time marches on
Towards the day's end
Another day's gone
Bringing us nearer our end.

But sometimes things happen
Things that are nice
Like the sunrise each morning
That makes us think twice.

S Tomlinson

COURTING DAYS
(From a lady's point of view)

The boy I loved
      Was billiards mad.
Courting days
      I never had.
All I heard was
      Pot that red.
In off the white
      That ball is dead
Sitting and watching
      Made me sigh.
And in bed
      I used to cry
Then my love
      Became unsure
For his habit
      Would not cure
Then one night
      I felt so blue
I hit him with
      His silly cue
This indeed
      Did the trick
Our love has
      Never run so thick
Remember ladies,
      Don't be beat
To get your man
      Just play it sweet.

Frank E Trickett

MISSING

you shouldn't have put me here
I say
I didn't ask for it

you should have been thinking
about me
about you
about us

I curl up

I started in noises
that you made
never thinking
I say

I turn over

silently

you think you can kill me
expel me
forget me

you can't

I suck my thumb

Glynis Charlton

DAD

The day will come when I will stand
At the entrance to that perfect land
And there to greet me will be my dad
Who will gently show me those wonders to come,
In that place where sunshine never ends
Where the shining waters flow
Through hills and valleys ever green,
Bathed in a golden glow,
And in those heavenly hills I'll find
The love and beauty that will always be mine,
And once again a Son I will be
To that dad I loved so tenderly.
You were always there for me
To help when times got rough.
You were the best friend I ever had,
And now you watch from heaven above,
I know you will always be with me,
No matter if it's day or night.
I know you will always help me,
With your guiding light.
I am so proud to call you my dad.

Carl Scottow

A NAIVE POEM

How naive was I?
I thought I could beat the system with brains.
Very naive!
My blood it runs red, not blue through my veins.

How naive was I?
I earned my degree with blood, sweat and tears.
Very naive!
I've lost every job to my southern peers.

How naive was I?
I thought I could cut off my working class roots.
Very naive!
My feet are tied tightly in steel toe-capped boots.

How naive was I?
I thought I had talent like Plath, Blake and Shelley.
Very naive!
I've put down my pen and switched on the telly.

Lucy McCollin

A Small Price To Pay

Another anniversary
With no one here to share
Next week would have been your birthday
But only I shall care

Sometimes you seem so very near
Is that your footstep in the hall?
Other days you are far away
As if you were never here at all

You may be at rest in some foreign grave
Tended by strangers you'd never met
But even though we seldom visit
You know we shall never forget

The homes with empty spaces
No passing time can fill
Youth and laughter missing
Emptiness and loneliness still

They went to do their duty
In a cause they thought was just
Now once a year for two minutes we remember them
Give thanks for what they left in trust

But we should never forget the debt
We owe to those so brave
Who gave up everything dear to them
Our country and way of life to save

So let us say a little prayer
Each day of thanks for them
Not only in November
Thanks for their sacrifice,

Amen

Peggy Hunter

CRYSTAL SKIES (CRYSTAL WATERS)

Ice shall freeze over the river
A warm sun will no longer rise
Leaves upon the trees shall wither
And all because of crystal skies.

Sheets of cold glass will cover lakes
The air will become cold and cruel
Grass will be hidden by snowflakes
And frozen shall be every pool.

All the flowers will become lost
Where a blanket of whiteness lies
And everything shall turn to frost
And all because of crystal skies

> Everything that nature brought us
> Will freeze around crystal waters.

Paul McIntyre

LIVE EACH MOMENT

When it's my turn to find
Such a bird on a wing
So free of restraints
And of life's little things
To live for the moment
And to never ever give in
To carry on laughing
And disguise every sin.

You look so alive
From this vision I see
So please look my way
So this world we can flee
Someone so loving
And free to choose when
A time in our lives
When we know we can win

Nobody seems perfect
From each life that gives in
So once in a while
We have to look deep, deep within
With questions inside,
We should never lose sight
The whole world in your eyes
We can dream of the life's fight.

Mark Lyons

ABC OF LIFE

Always kinder than necessary,
Burying sorrow to let it rest,
Cleaning out all the negativity,
Devotes its life to give its best,

Each day to live as if the last,
Forgives before a sorry is said,
Giving freely to all on its path.
Helping each other to achieve,

Illuminates the heart with love,
Joyfully receiving from others,
Keeping its mind in the present,
Loving enemies like brothers,

Makes good cheer last all year
Never sleeps on man's unrest,
Open its heart to let go of fear,
Prays for peace in the world,

Questions if it sees a wrong,
Revises thoughts of jealousy,
Saturates its mind with a song,
Takes the time for all it sees,

Unconditionally gives its love,
Volunteers help as its occupation,
Walks its path with utmost calm,
X-ray visions volatile situations,

Yields to come back stronger,
Zooms to help all in trouble,

ABC of how to live this life,
Learning the rules to live,
To end hardship and strife,
With love to give and give.

Teresa Wild

BRONTËLAND VISIT

Scents from early autumn fires,
As blue smoke rises,
Fragrant, holding a promise,
Of more fine, warm days.

Walking past fields of seedlings,
Like cotton wool shrouds,
Protecting next time's blooming,
Drifting on the breeze.

Reaching the tea shop, cool, dim,
Blue ware, picture plates,
Cats sleeping in the corners,
The tables set.

Cups rattle as tea is sipped,
Jugs hang from dark beams,
Haworth is a pleasant place,
With a history.

Beyond the shop is moorland,
Haunted by the ghosts,
Of literary lovers,
Hungrily searching.

Her white face is pressed against,
Imaginary,
Windowpane, does she seem real?
Mortal lovers pass.

Outside with faraway eyes,
Believing themselves,
Literary romantics,
For a few hours.

Kathleen Mary Scatchard

IT'S MONDAY

You wake late in the morning,
And you think the clock is fast,
You think it's nearly seven,
But it's almost quarter past,
Your dressing gown is inside out,
You fight to get it on,
And then you see one slipper,
Where has the other gone?
You make it to the bathroom,
Someone pipped you at the post,
And when you finally get down,
They've eaten all the toast.

Constance Bellard

Your Mum

Y ou never know how much you miss them
   until they have finally gone
O ur lives are never quite the same
   without our Special Mum
U ntil their last day comes along
   and their deeds upon this Earth are done
R est assured they are in heaven, at peace
   and reunited with their loved ones

M any times you'll wonder
   why it had to be
   you'll find that peace within you,
   as time eventually heals

U nder no circumstances
   would she want you
   sad and full of woe
   she'll be with you forever
   she's in your heart you know
   she was a 'Special Lady'
   who'll never be replaced
   you're left with treasured memories of a
M other that was loved and praised . . .

C A Walker

YOUTH AND LOVE

What is this thing we call growing old,
Where days are long and nights are cold.
Faltering memories living in the past,
Of those yesteryears gone by too fast.
Youthful bodies through time are spent,
Lined and gnarled, tired and bent.
Callused hands from toiling each day,
Misshapen fingers with pain that won't go away.
Unseeing eyes, once sparkled bright,
Scanning the open door, hoping for sight,
Of the face of a loved one, familiar and dear,
Pretending we've not been forgotten this year.
Wouldn't it be wonderful, if only we could,
Bring back those years of youth and love?

Rita M Arksey

TO THE BOSS

I shall be a long time dead
Yet you begrudge me life
You must demand demand demand
You invent interminable complaints
Insatiable in your appetite
For my labour, my possessions my heart my mind
My breath
And yet of course and yet
You say I have no call upon yourself
For even as the sun shines
And the butterfly settles on the buddleia
Even as the lavender pulses with its fragrance
Begging to be smelt as well as seen
Even as night-scented stock and honeysuckle
Tuck the sun to bed to close a perfect day
From sight to smell to touch
The senses seeking their own transcendence
Yet you are always there
Carping grasping greeding out my life
Already calculating by whom and when and where
And of course at what minimum cost to you
I can be replaced
Once my usefulness is done
You are a parasite
Though powerful
A parasite nonetheless
I shall be a long time dead
Yet you begrudge me life.

Nicholas Howard

ACCIDENT

I popped out for hoover bags one day
I got in my car ready to go
Told my daughter
'I'll only be ten minutes or so.'

Shop did not have any, but on the way home
Came out of a side road
Waited for the van to pass
I was nearly home again at last.

Big van was stopping
It was in front
Put its left indicator on
It was going to stop
I checked my mirror for anything behind
'Go round the van,'
Was the thought in my mind.

Put my indicator on, round I went
But man in van
Turned right into my car
I screamed, I cried, I was hurting too
My dog was alright, she wanted a ride
'I thought I'd killed her,' I cried.

Ambulance came, police came too
Police got my daughter
Lots of questions, they asked
They were not very sympathetic
They were getting my daughter mad

Left at hospital for hours on my own
Crying and shaking, very cold too
It just wasn't good enough but this is all true.

Driver of van said he was guilty
Police said 'Oh no, he's not.'
They said it was me that was really guilty
Is this a terrible plot, I thought a lot.

Many months passed
To prove I was innocent, I'm glad to say
My nerves have been shattered
But there's one thing I find
I'll never go out for hoover bags again.
The memory of it
Will never leave my mind.

Trisha Moreton

A LONGING FOR SCENIC LOCATIONS

Wind in the hills and sun up in the sky,
And graceful weeping willow trees that weep but never sigh.
A body of water flows aimlessly across the dell,
It creates many ripples yet not a swell.
Many bushes and blooms perfume the air,
A picturesque scenery bringing about a common stare.
Many unperturbable seeking people travel when the day is hot,
Hastily heading for a breathtaking beauty spot.

John P Evans

YOU STOLE MY WHOLE LIFE

It hurts very much there. It was you who put it there.
Breaking all the boundaries without a care.
You penetrated me in that bed. All this pain, my blood shed.
Locked in dark dungeons, evils unfold.
You stole my virginity, childhood, teens, parenthood, freedom.
My whole life, You simply had no such rights.
You rooted
consisting excruciations of deep depressions, anxieties,
personality disorders, anti-social behaviours. Suicide.
Deep betrayals of trust, deep fears, addictions, self-hatreds,
no identity, sadness and conflicting tears.
It is you to blame for all this shame.
It is you to blame for all my pains.
You invaded
my bones, bloodstream, hair and skin. You invaded everything.
From birth, childhood, teens, middle age and old.
All these years abuse still unfolds.
I believed you had stolen everything. You could not steal more.
Then you invaded my life again, kept on stealing more.
I discovered
meditations, meridian lines, vortexes, chakras, earth rays, healings.

Revealings
of God, Jesus, Holy Mother.
Their sacred and spiritual healings.
I discovered
unfound truths and strengths from those sacred revealings.
You, my perpetrator, unbalanced the universe.
Your soul is not retrieved,
Reincarnations in adverse, you get what you have achieved.

Jenifer Ellen Austin

A DEPRESSING TALE

Depression is the darkest hole,
Devouring heart, and mind, and soul.
The deepest pit, a lonely place,
Depression has no friendly face.
A numbing void, the twilight zone,
A place to dwell in fear, alone!
Where nothing helps to ease the pain,
Of incessant drumming in the brain.
Tears flow freely, oft unbidden,
As feelings rise from deep, once hidden.
Lost, out of touch, bereft,
Death, often, the only exit left!
When triumph lies in daily survival,
Until new strength permits revival.
Though despair is never far away,
The depressive just lives from day to day!

Brian L Porter

THE WAR WIDOW

I wed and I gave my maiden years
To one who loved me in return
Now dead in a grave near Armentieres
His lifeless stay is no sojourn.

They say he died that we might live
But how can I redeem the pledge I gave?
This country has no cheer to give
Those wives who comforted the brave.

Forgotten are the ones who lost
Security and love their lives to span
Forgotten, but still we pay the cost
Forgotten, like my forgotten man.

Charles Meacher

ART OF RELIGION

Experience equals wisdom,
making the mind free for
constructive action,
an action to teach the human heart,
the sympathies of drama,
it's sincere, tolerant and kindness,
of creation,
from one's own image,
taught towards the delight of economic
mind,
to visualise ideas,
whether the outcome is a success or
a failure,
to discard the selection of the worthless,
shake free of realism,
give nothing more or less,
than one is deserved,
but look in the mirror to find the answer.
Although in the mirror is not the change,
it's in the mind of those who look in it.

A E Holland (17)

WHY WE WON'T FORGET YOU

Hornsea means so much to me,
This little town beside the sea
When weekends come we wend our way
Weary from work, we come here to play

But when we came in springtime,
Our pleasure turned to pain
The centre of this little town
Would never be the same

The open space, the air, the grace,
The very feeling of this place
Had been destroyed for sake of gain
What price to pay - we can't reclaim
What Hornsea had that made us glad,
Now replacing good with bad
Has made us angry, but mostly sad

And so before we go back home
We'll gaze upon this scene
At the spot where the old beech stood,
And ponder what might have been

We'll remember how we used to sit beneath its shady bower
To shelter from the summer sun or from an April shower
And we'll never forget that beautiful tree
In Hornsea betwixt the mere and the sea.

Polly Worsdale

YOU AND I OR VICE VERSA

It's like a yo-yo.
Is it the old heave-ho?
You and I.
Is it goodbye?
You and he,
I and she,
You and they,
With not a trace
Of regret -
Or is there?

I know I have
To share you
But I cannot bear
To lose you.

Give me a ring,
Ding-dong,
Ping-pong -
Any game
You like.

Clive Williams

LAST OF THE DORIAN

'Twas at the break of dawn,
Seas calm against a cloudless sky.
They stood silent on that fateful morn
And watched the waves roll by.

Young Meg wept for the father she had lost.
Where was God on the tragic night?
Morning sadly saw the cost
When all hands were lost by morning light.

Enraging seas and ceaseless wind
Had lashed against the shore,
When lurching home from distant lands
The Dorian's crew could withstand no more.

The moon was the colour of newly-shed blood
As by the headland villagers helplessly stood.
Wild bells rang out from nearby church tower
And told of disaster at that dreadful hour.
The storm clouds scurried above raging seas
But heeded not the loved ones' pleas.

Ensuing days have seen
An azure sky and calm seas of green.
These sailors taken to their ocean bed
Must be enshrined for their courage
In the annals of the dead.

Dorothy Sheard

DISAPPEAR

I wish I could erase myself
like a pointless word from a page
or reverberate between two cliffs
as an echo would, then fade away.

Whisper my name into the wind
and let it gently blow away.
Let the rain wash over my steps
and hide the journey that I've made.

Pluck me from the place I fill
undo the acts I've done.
Take away the words I've said,
remove memories one by one.

I want to leave no epitaph
on a slab or stone to mourn
cremate these, my final words
and forget that I was born.

Susan Smith

MS - MY STRUGGLE

I got up one morning and found I couldn't walk
I had lost my balance, slurring when trying to talk
Panic and hysteria were racing through my mind
As I was admitted to hospital - what would they find?
After tests and a scan, the Consultant said 'Yes,
I'm afraid you have definitely got MS!
Don't be disparaged and don't get too upset
Put wheelchairs right out of your mind, there's hope for you yet.'

After months of physio and tears of frustration
I eventually won through with sheer determination
I can walk again now albeit slightly lame
And my lifestyle has changed, it will never be the same
So when life is a struggle as it often is
I just remember my doctor telling me this
'Don't give up and stay positive'
These words will stay with me for as long as I live.

S Pontefract

IF WE RULED THE WORLD

Why do humans grumble so much
And blame God for all that goes wrong?
When He gives a wonderful touch
In the home and in the throng.

What if God gave up in despair
And said, 'I am fed up with you,'
There would be nobody to really care,
Whatever would you and I do?

Suppose also that He stopped the sun
And the rain too from falling down,
Perhaps we would not have much fun
And the grass and trees would be brown.

If He stopped the creatures great and small
From giving their pleasure to us
Even giraffes which grow very tall,
We would all kick up such a fuss.

If we made time, it would be good
To find how much we have to treasure,
How God supplies our daily food
And gives us all so much pleasure.

So let's stop grumbling and just give praise
For a God who is faithful and true
To all of us in the human race,
And thank Him every day too.

Vera G Taylor

DECANTER COLLARS

How many gallons
Have the metal labels
Seen poured?
How many salons
One hears of in fables
Can one afford
To go into,
Offer the gin to
Be frisky with whisky
Hurry the sherry
And, though far gone, sup port?
Is it then a surprise
When feet, knees and thighs
Can no longer support?

Richard Birch

SUMMER SUNSET FROM PINDER'S FIELD

Late evening sun dazzling in the western sky
Slowly courses lower in the heavens,
Beyond the steeple of St. Barnabas,
Far from lofty splendour of dale-spanning arches
And distant miles of Pennine hills.
His bright rays point the way to crystal spheres
And lead to remote, mythical Elysian Fields,
Whilst streaming downward seem
To touch the tips of highest peaks.

He orchestrates his descent in an
Unleashed flood of lustrous yellows.
As the heavens unveil a crowning
Ribbon of rainbow greenness,
The flaring orb, essence of all earthly life,
Vanishes from the eternal scene in a spectacular finale
Creating in its wake boundless sweeps of flame and gold.
A rising tide in faintest pink unfolds, filling
The firmament with an ocean of deepest sunset rose.

A drifting cloud briefly appears
As an ethereal spangled city,
Its wispy satellites are islands
In a calmly-glistening celestial sea
Awash with mystic tints that stretch
To an infinity of lonely horizons.

Azalea sunset fires grow dim and fade
In an all-enveloping afterglow of violet shades.
Misting hills and moorland softly merge;
Waters of the Wharfe that glowed under a sundown sky
Gleam steely-grey in the gathering dusk;
Cropped grasses of the pasture are palely tinged.
Lights like dying candles glide over
Shadowed symmetry of the sandstone bridge,
To be lost below sombre contours of the Crag.

All enchantment gone, the transient clouds disperse
Toward twilight of the eastern plain;
The sky darkens and earth awaits
The silence of the night.

Ethel Wade

LEAVING

Fallen leaves; a fire sleeping.
Dry as snakes they tempt her eyes,
crimson, ochre, copper, bronze -
sunlight snared when summer dies.

Overhead, a thread of swallow
earth and air together weaves,
head and heart: yet she sits, weeping.
Tears scald when love deceives.

Sunlit in October silence,
there, among the leaves, she lies
wrought by winds of winter's warning
loosened from the silk-screen skies.

Absolute and elemental
she who wept no longer grieves.
Crimson. Ochre. Copper. Bronze.
Now she thinks in fallen leaves.

Allison Bond

MY DREAM

My dream is a garden, caressed by the sun,
A place I can sit when my day's work is done.
Where pink, and blue hyacinth bloom in the Spring,
Where perfume and beauty surround me to bring
Peace and tranquillity, hope from despair,
Whilst birds hop around me - of blue tits a pair -
A red-breasted robin to cheer me along,
A blackbird to sing me his sweet-noted song.

In tending my garden, I'll while away hours,
My dreams will be endless in sweet-scented bowers;
There'll be roses of yellow, deep pink, purest white,
Rich lavender borders enhancing delight:
Most fragrant, some fragile - like delicate lace,
Carnation and poppy, a pansy whose face
I'll lift 'twixt my fingers, its outline I'll trace;
There'll be thyme in the crevices, sweet-scented stocks,
Rosemary and lupin and tall hollyhocks.

So you may espy me at daybreak or dusk,
Engrossed in their beauty, enthralled when I touch
The softness of petal, the vein of a leaf . . .
At dawn there'll be harebells - fairies beneath!
I'll work in my garden, treasure it too,
Enjoying its pleasures, alone, or with you.

Eunice M Caines

SEASIDE THOUGHTS

Sunny days and misty nights
On our way to northern lights.

Sitting here and drinking tea
We'll watch the bathers in the sea.

Football games on sandy beaches
See the children with ice cream faces.

The joy of Peasholm (Park) we can't fake
While rowing around the boating lake.

Crazy golf and ghost train rides
From the Prom we'll watch the tide.

We'll eat our local fish and chips
Then hop on a bus for an evening trip.

Board the train to Scalby Mills,
Through the Park and beyond yon hill.

Penny Arcades, with bingo calls
Speedboat rides, and seafood stalls.

Castle walks and harbour strolls
Our seaside break has us enthralled.

From the Spa to the corner cafe,
You and I will have a laugh.

Sunny days and misty nights,
We're here at last by the seaside lights.

David Townend

IMPRESSIONS BY THE SEA

Saturday, 31st October, 1998 (8am)

High, so high the seagulls fly
Soaring in the bright blue sky
See the sunlight on their wings
They really are such wondrous things
They woke me up in the early dawn
Welcoming another morn
These are the joys the seaside brings
It's no wonder my heart sings

Saturday, (11am)

I sit and watch, the show is free
One more performance just for me.

Sunday, 1st November 1998

The seagulls cry and so do I
Because we now must say goodbye
They will still the skyways roam
Whilst I must pack, and go back home
Yet, when I visit here, once more
I know they will do an encore.

Tuesday, 29th December 1998

I am back here once more
Oh, so close to the seashore
And the seagulls have again
Started once more, to entertain
High in the cloudy sky they soar
To background sounds of waves on shore
In the wind, they bank and glide
And my great pleasure, I cannot hide.

Joyce Metcalfe

ELEANOR PROTHEROE

Perhaps it was I who unwittingly caused Miss Protheroe's
comical habit:
One morning I gave her a lettuce I'd grown - so Eleanor purchased
a rabbit!
She drew out her savings that bright afternoon (for hutches are
rather expensive)
And bought the most sumptuous cage she could find - the rabbit was
quite apprehensive!

And then in the market one blustery day some tins were being sold
very cheaply -
They'd all lost their labels and some of them, too, were battered and
dinted quite deeply;
Yet they were a bargain, that can't be denied (Miss Protheroe truly
was smitten)
We found that they all contained 'Pussy Cat Purr' and so she
adopted a kitten!

Well next, at a jumble sale Eleanor saw a glass bowl that she had
a wish for,
She bought it and went to the Pet Shop to show what *now* she must
purchase a fish for:
Now that meant, of course, she must redecorate her walls and replace
every curtain,
For all had to tone with the bright orange fish (of that she was
totally certain).

No sooner had Eleanor finished the task, she went to a shop in the city
And spied there a sofa, reduced by a third, that she thought
remarkably pretty:
The sofa, of course, didn't fit her abode - Miss Protheroe drafted a letter
Requiring the House Agents, find her a home that suited her
furniture better!

The Fashion Boutique had reduced all its stock, Miss Protheroe noticed
with pleasure,
She entered and purchased a gaudy blue frock and proudly she showed
me her treasure:

That night, in the Greedy Pig Restaurant, she commanded they feed her
with plenty:
'You see,' she explained, 'I must put on some weight - that dress is an
outsize, a twenty!'

The season was ending and Sales had begun, and something was
making me nervous
Miss Protheroe purchased a white satin gown, designed by a grand
nuptial service!
Well, Eleanor hadn't a suitor in tow, so off to the town she was heading,
To pay a large fee to a Marriage Bureau - and soon I attended
her wedding!

When she had been married a year and a day she went into Bunty
McGradle's
Where free gifts were offered of garments and toys to all who were
purchasing cradles;
I heard she had been to the doctor one day and later she came
to me shyly:
'I think I can guess what you're going to say,' I said as I smiled
at her slyly.

It now seems imperative that she stays home (we're doing our utmost
to make her)
You see, there's an offer that's just been announced by Pringle, the
town's undertaker
If anyone books for a funeral *now*, declares the lugubrious Pringle,
He'll throw in a large double coffin, it seems, for only the price
of a single!

Rosemary Yvonne Vandeldt

SOULMATES

Where are you?
Gone without trace!

Even your face
Dims in my mind.
How can I find
The peace that came
When I spoke your name
In my last greeting,
At our last meeting?

Four times we met, in company,
I and you, you and me.
Nearer we drew,
Until we knew
Our rendezvous
Was déjà vu.

Sweetheart? Lover?
Sister? Brother?
Lost and found,
Eternally bound,
Yet parted again.
Biding till when
Our time is due.

But where are you?

Louie Carr

HOLKHAM HALL
(1st August, 2000)

Palladian palace,
Perfect for perambulatory peregrinations.
Holkham.

'Twix obelisks, and the sea to the north
Curvaceous drives between mature trees,
Minds may drift back to centuries ago
When carriages were driven with wigged passengers.
Did they wander through the parkland?
Did they venture to the sea and onto the 'beach'?
Did they swim and make sandcastles?
Or confine themselves to the terrace,
The formal gardens beneath vaulted windows?
Would they now rise up and revolt
Against the tourist throng,
Sailing upon their lake,
Regarding their agricultural wares,
Walking through their corridored temple?

Do we, with envy stare
At their achievement,
Or simply eat our ice cream
And moan at the entrance charge?

T Huntington

OUR HOLLY

On the morn that you were born
you had a sleepy eye
I first glanced your fluffy blonde hair
as you began to cry.
The TV was playing Bon Jovi on the
American Top Ten
When I recall life's happy moments
I think of the tune now and then.
I shall always remember the moment
how we fell for your little charms
The tears of love ran down Daddy's face
as he held you in his arms.
When you first saw your brothers, Steven and Scott
they were so kind and protective of you
They watched over your clumsy moments
and everything you'd do.
Now your schooldays have come around
and we have to learn to let go
Of our darling little angel
a schoolgirl now you know.
Throughout your life you have brought us joy
much happiness and a few tears
Borne out of the love within our hearts
for our Holly through the years.
Wherever life may take you
may all your dreams come true
Just as they did for us all
when God chose us for you.

Michele Simone Fudge

PAST TIMES

So here we are! 2000 years
Not without our hopes and fears
To space we've been and moon too
Achievements just, for me and you
We travel round to places far
By bus and plane and car
Computers now have come our way
Such clever things are here to stay
People live not in their land
And travel far for sea and sand
Who can see what's next to come
A magic world for all, not some
So put a smile upon your face
With a hearty cheer for the human race.

S Towse

SONNET FOR THE SINGLE GIRL

Contrary to modern thinking
Being single's rather nice.
No one to impress with housework;
No one giving out advice.
At the weekend, if I want to
I can stay in bed all day
Reading, drinking tea and farting
In a rather sluttish way.
Alternatively, I can go out
Straight from work without a care.
Stagger home at five next morning,
No explanations, who or where.
No debates on what's for dinner
Or what to watch on the TV.
When I get up in the morning
I know that all the post's for me.
And if I ever ponder on my choice
I think of 'Football Focus', and rejoice.

Jill Burdall

CHILDHOOD

Listen to the wind swaying the grass
The blackbird sing at dawn
Watch the lonely moon float through the sky
They speak to you and I.
Listen to nature calling you
Run through the windswept grass
See the swaying hawthorn climb
Swim the placid lake
Seas and mountains call to you
Feel free, one day you'll be a man.

Irene Patricia Kelly

HYDRAMUM

There is a keen gard'ner of York
      goes frantic
            at sight of a stalk

'Mother,' said Daughter
      'Watch it, you oughta
he's after your head
      then, if you're not dead
you'll find you have many instead.'

Ottoline Fryer

JOHN

You did say 'Wait' so that's what I'll do,
I always do what you tell me to.
(Well nearly always, anyway.)
So here I am and here I stay.
But I can't help wondering, you know
How slowly the waiting moments go.
Those things that bang on the wall and tick
Are nothing more than a shabby trick;
They measure time by the turn of a wheel,
But I think time is the ache I feel,
Somewhere inside me when you're away
When a lonely minute's as long as a day
And a day is a desert because we're apart
Time is measured, I'm sure by the heart
In spite of the pendulum's idle chatter
When we're together time doesn't matter.

Ada Tye

SILENT TEARS

A child sheds tears on the street corner
No one around. So lonely out there
Broken, bruised and hurt
Cold, alone, afraid
Not knowing a warm loving word
A child whose world is to fight to survive
To feed on the slops of humankind
No pity or sympathy is shared
This child wants empathy
Just to be cared for.

A broken milk bottle stands
In a pool of blood
Where the child stood, just moments ago

Cowering, running scared
The child goes into hiding
A sanctuary of their silent world
No words are spoken
Just cold empty tears
A child so full of fear
With no one there

One day you might see this child
And not know that you could have seen them
Could you have helped
The child stem their silent tears.

Jane Reed

THE FIRST DAY WITHOUT YOU

The day stretched before me empty
All purpose completely gone
I wanted to cry like a baby
But for my son I had to be strong

I tried to distract him with games
To pretend like I didn't care
It didn't feel right to him either
For he too knew that you were not there

I know others feel this way too
Thousands of us in the same boat
Desperately clock watching obsessively
Waiting for the time to get our coat

Do you miss me too?
Is the void and the ache something we share?
Or are you too involved with new things
To notice that we are not there?

I know soon it will be over
Time to paint on a smile and act cool
Even though my life is forever changed
Following your first day at school.

Karen Naylor

THE GYPSY MAN

He has a caravan, horse and windows two,
The caravan has a chimney, the smoke coming through,
He has a rosy cheeked wife, a little baby brown,
The gypsy family travel from town to town.

The roads are long and winding the sea green,
Their house on wheels, can be a bathing machine,
The world is wide and far, and they ride,
Rumbling and splashing, reaching the other side.

Chairs to mend, he shouts, pegs to sell,
He bangs metal basins, like a bell,
Selling baskets, trays and painted plates,
I'd like to travel with him, how I'd love to roam.

Wm G Whalley

TWO YEAR SENTENCE

'Twas on a sunny day that servitude began.
We came, a variegated crew, into the grey stone station,
Drew our last breaths of freedom, then passed reluctantly outside.
Herded into trucks by bellowing soldiery, clutching our
                                            pitiful possessions,
We rattled off to conscript service, isolated now from normal life.

Inside the camp, desolate on tank rutted moor,
We occupied uncomfortable huts,
Parcelled up civilian clothes to send back home,
Donned itchy khaki, knowing there was no escape.
We had begun our two year sentence.

That night, a young recruit beside me wept.
For six weeks there were no more sunny days.

Peter Hicks

A STRANGE PRESENT

Autumn usually starts in April,
Well, it always seems to here,
Where two holly trees stand together,
For early leaf fall every year.

There's an old friend I rely on,
To clear up the unwanted mess.
He's big and strong, in orange plastic,
Electric, I must confess.

Out he comes, my pal, Leaf Hoover,
To work, in his mechanical way,
Sucking up the natural litter
From paths and flower beds, each day.

By July the holly trees have finished,
But some others, across the street,
Begin to prepare for autumn,
Scattering waste around my feet.

Amid the lovely blooms of summer,
When the garden is at its best,
Crumpled bits of sycamore and chestnut,
Put my good temper to the test.

Increasing through August and September,
By October they reach their peak,
So me and my invaluable Leaf Hoover,
Clean up seven days of the week.

By November Leaf Hoover is exhausted,
But I need him way past Bonfire Night.
In December he gets his Christmas present:
I hang him in the garage, out of sight.

We part our company for the winter,
When I sweep up errant leaves with a brush,
While Leaf Hoover has a well-deserved retirement,
To prepare him for the next year's April rush.

Lorna Lea

THE MAGIC OF THE YORKSHIRE DALES

The Dales in the spring are a wonderful sight.
The lambs in the fields skip and play.
Their mothers, the ewes, saunter slowly along.
They've nothing to do all the day.

The colourful meadows and murmuring streams;
The beautiful rivers that flow;
The waterfalls rush, roaring, smelling of spray
And pound to the rivers below.

In summer the beautiful valleys are full
Of flowers that perfume the air.
The cowslips so yellow reflect the sun's rays.
The buzzing bees are everywhere.

The splendour of autumn is grand to behold.
Magnificent forests in browns
And tans and golds, russets, mahoganies, reds
And heather in bloom on the downs.

The Dales in the winter are a wonderland.
Spectacular snow covered trees
And moors sparkle under the cloudless blue sky.
No jewels can compare with these.

Joyce M Turner

UNDERSTANDING THAT YOU LOVE ME

Understanding that you love me is the hardest thing I've known,
But now I know our love will last for ever.
Your love for me is precious, as is my love for you,
And our love for each other will never fade.

My nights are long and lonely without you by my side
Knowing I need you more each passing day.
For without you beside me to share the love I feel
The endless nightmares will never go away.

I wish we were together, right now, to join in our love
For I want so much to show my love for you,
And tell you it will last forever, as will your love for me,
Then we will be together for ever more.

Ashley K Howard

ENVIRONMENT

Although my time on Earth, is drawing to its close,
I prayed to leave, seeing hope and vision rife,
all respecting nature. The air. A butterfly at the rose,
so many things, provided with this gift of life.

Many are disappearing now, through human greed.
War pestilence and famine anticipated as normal,
selfishness, jealousy, and falsehood an accepted creed,
disease and unnecessary death, a happening informal.

It is beyond understanding, so much can be thrown away,
and warnings about the future, brushed aside.
Tamper further with the air we need today,
It is certain, no further life, will, in this world abide.

Maurice Wilkinson

TUTANKHAMUN

(Kiss = gentle bite to hand, or the same to face without the bite.)

King Tut, my cat, has perfect ways
to show his love throughout our days.
His 'Mmmm-alarm' on morning bed
just gently says: 'When sleep has fled,
it's time for praise and not to laze.'

He purrs, soft-pats, side-rolls, and pays
his deepest love with kiss: then plays.
Who joyously rubs head to head?
King Tut, my cat.

When gardening, he always stays
by me to gaze; and later, lays
dead mice in shed (or house instead!)
'Love-gifts for you,' is clearly said.
Sheathed goodnight - paws to face he'll raise:
King Tut; sleep well.

Tony Hughes-Southwart

SCREWED UP

Her father drank
Her uncle touched
And in between
There was nothing much!

She had to cope
She had to manage
She had to prove
They'd done no damage

And to others
She convinced them all
Her head held high
She'd walk so tall.

But deep inside
She must of knew
As she got older
Her feelings were few

Her uncle stopped touching
Her father still drank
But she'd left home now
Only herself to thank

A calmer environment
A relaxed atmosphere
But how do you adapt
After so many years?

She was used to the shouting
Felt at unease with the calm
She felt very anxious
Aware of the harm

Married with children
Still desperate to rid
Those lingering memories
Of life as a kid!

Julie Robinson

POEM ABOUT BRIDLINGTON

Bridlington is the number one resort for me,
because it's bright and breezy to live by the sea.
Tourists would come to lay in the sun
And have fun in the pubs when the long day is done.
A warm welcome awaits you in our friendly seaside town,
And everyday is a perfect day and never a need to frown.
When the season is over and Christmas approaches.
The town and hotels prepare for visiting coaches
the shops dress their windows and streets filled with lights.
Their is an air of excitement and children's delights.

Ian Burdekin

SACRIFICIAL ROAD

Scanty merchandise
Parading ancient rituals,
Offering a choice of flavours
For the discerning taste.

Homemakers witness
Live action television,
Viewing through window sets
With no licence required.

Curtains draw together
Forming truth tight controls,
Curious children switch on
Revealing forbidden programmes.

Respectability cruises by
Scanning the morsels on offer,
Strutting victims anticipating
Partaking as dish of the day.

Glenn Granter

2000 AD WAS IT ALL WE THOUGHT

Was it all we thought? This year of stars galore
With all the talk of years gone by and many tales of Yore
When it first began a promised peace by every man
Each nation played her part to draft God's plan and make a start!
The Millennium now in motion, each heart would gladly open.

Did it bring an end to hunger, war, and pain
The same old resolutions again were made in vain!
As the century before the year started with such hope
Man's dreams once more were shattered as 'hatred' ran amok

The holding of the hands of man a mere 'joke' a misread plan
And as 2000, soon will close
We'll use the same old worn out prose
All pray for peace, God hears he knows
It's in your hands 'The future's yours'

So don your happy new year mask!
Try 'keep' the promise you take to task
And make each 'peace talk' and 'cease fire' last!

Angela Maria Wilson

A MYSTERY TRIP

On a sunny, summer night,
We set off for a ride,
To view the many wonders
Of our Dales countryside.

My husband happy at the helm,
Leaves busy roads, behind,
As up the narrow, twisting tracks,
Our vehicle will wind.

Occasionally we meet a car,
Towards the ditch we go,
I hold my breath,
And how we miss a scrape I'll never know.

Miles and miles we travel,
No signposts can be seen,
But only undulating hills,
Wild moors and fields of green.

When we get home our family asks,
Which places did you view?
I scratch my head and then reply,
'I haven't got a clue.'

Elaine Beresford

malignant sadness

too many life-shocks
have discharged my soul,
a barren, hopeless future of
empty, featureless salt flats
inhospitable, but inviting
malignant sadness

dreams all gone
no motivation,
burnt out with stress
i sleep for days at a time,
too miserable to live with
malignant sadness

once husband, step-father,
son-in-law, brother,
uncle, friend, lover,
colleague, provider,
now no role to play in
malignant sadness

pointlessly walking in
bustling city centre,
i burst into tears
for no more reason
than black, overwhelming,
malignant sadness

'one day at a time'
is their best advice,
but meaningless, daily survival
does not create life,
only another 24 hours of
malignant sadness

p kemp

CIRCLE OF DREAMS

I am told if you write down your wishes
Then one day, it's said, they'll come true
So beware what you dream or perhaps it will seem
Like a thunderbolt out of the blue
For perhaps it would be a mixed blessing
If all that we wanted we gained
If we asked, and received, never learned how to grieve
Never learned what it was to restrain
Then how could our characters flourish
What strengths could we possibly bring
To a world that can wither and perish
When we're longing to teach it to sing
Though we all have our dreams and our visions
Yet long may we each bear our strife
For only by this, may we treasure the bliss
Which can come, and can colour our life.

Judy Smith

HOURS OF OURS

I want an hour,
To be ours
Then I want hours,
To be ours.
I want hours,
Of us.
I want hours,
Of our laughter.
I want hours,
Of our bodies;
Entwining.
I want hours,
Of our lips;
Parting.
I want an hour.
To be ours.

Rachel C Zaino